## G. SCHIRMER'S COLLECTION OF OPERA LIBRETTOS

# SIMON BOCCANEGRA

Melodrama in Three Acts and a Prologue

Music by

## *Giuseppe Verdi*

Text by

### FRANCESCO MARIA PIAVE

(Based on the drama by Antonio Garcia Gutiérrez with modifications by Arrigo Boito)

English Version by

MARY ELLIS PELTZ

Ed. 2586

# G. SCHIRMER, Inc.

DISTRIBUTED BY

HAL•LEONARD®
CORPORATION

7777 W. BLUEMOUND RD. P.O. BOX 13819 MILWAUKEE, WI 53213

# SIMON BOCCANEGRA

The opera is based on a play by the Spaniard, Antonio Garcia Gutiérrez, also author of *El Trovador* and formerly Spanish consul at Genoa, where he seems to have become interested in the romantic personality of the ex-pirate who became Doge. The composer, Giuseppe Verdi, already had eighteen operas to his credit when, at the age of forty-four, he entrusted the libretto of *Boccanegra* to Francesco Piave in order to fulfill a contract made the previous year with the Fenice Theatre at Venice.

The premiere, which took place on March 12, 1857, was characterized by the composer as "almost a greater fiasco than *Traviata*" although the work was praised by the critics for "its beautiful melodies and profound philosophy." The opposition of the public was repeated later at Milan though partly reversed at Naples.

Verdi's faith in the opera is indicated by his defense of Piave and his opinion that "a higher standard of performance and a public really willing to listen" might be needed to make it successful. Twenty years later he decided to revise the score and induced Arrigo Boito to modify the text, bringing the villain's poisoning of the Doge's wine cup onto the stage and improving the first act finale. Verdi's alterations were more radical and include a new sombre prelude and opening scene, the introduction to the first act, the splendid scene of the council chamber and the last act wedding choruses.

The revised version was first presented on March 24, 1881, in Milan, only six years before Verdi's final tragic work and greatest masterpiece, *Otello,* which, in many respects, it is said to resemble.

# THE STORY

PROLOGUE. In 1339 the people of Genoa, weary of factional warfare between the Guelphs and Ghibellines, created the office of Doge to help consolidate the Genoese republic. Paolo and Pietro, leaders of the People's Party, plot to obtain the power of the aristocracy by electing the popular corsair, Simone Boccanegra, as puppet Doge. Boccanegra accepts their proposal so that he may marry Maria, daughter of the noble Jacopo Fiesco, who has imprisoned her ever since she bore Boccanegra's child. After a mob of commoners, incited by Pietro, pledges support of the corsair's cause, Fiesco emerges from his palace to the square, mourning Maria's death. Unaware of the tragedy, Boccanegra asks his friendship, but the implacable old man demands to be given his granddaughter. Boccanegra laments that the child has disappeared and despairing of further talk rushes into the deserted palace and finds Maria's casket. As he comes out a mob hails him as Doge.

ACT I. Twenty-five years have passed. In the garden of the Grimaldi palace, where the embittered Fiesco now lives in hiding under the pseudonym Andrea, his ward Amelia awaits her lover, Gabriele Adorno, who has joined Fiesco in a plot to overthrow Boccanegra. When the youth enters she tells him that the Doge wishes her to marry Paolo; at once Gabriele seeks out Fiesco to obtain the old man's blessing for himself. Suddenly Boccanegra arrives and in an interview with Amelia discovers that she is his long-lost daughter. The guardian in whose care he had placed her had died; the child had wandered to a convent where she had taken the place of the true Amelia Grimaldi, recently dead, so that the wealth of the exiled Grimaldi might not be confiscated but remain in the hands of the family. When Boccanegra learns that his daughter loves Gabriele, he refuses to give her to Paolo, who kidnaps her. While negotiating a treaty between Genoa and Venice in his council chamber, the Doge is interrupted by shouts in the streets. He bravely admits the unruly mob that has captured both Fiesco, who goes unrecognized, and Gabriele, who defiantly charges Boccanegra with Amelia's abduction and tries to stab him. Amelia herself rushes in and throws herself between them. She pleads with the Doge to forgive Gabriele, who suspects she is Boccanegra's mistress, and describes her abduction, hinting at Paolo's complicity. The Doge quiets the raging spectators and commands Paolo, as a state official, to curse the man who plotted this infamy. Sick with horror, he does so and rushes from the hall as the assembly repeats his curse. Fiesco and Gabriele are sent to prison.

ACT II. In the Doge's apartment, Paolo pours poison into Boccanegra's drinking bowl. Summoning Fiesco from his cell he vainly urges the old man to assassinate Boccanegra. Next he incites Gabriele to fury with insinuations as to the Doge's relationship with Amelia. When the youth is left to his thoughts, Amelia enters, but before she can explain to Gabriele that the Doge is her father, Boccanegra follows. Gabriele hides in the balcony. Amelia asks her father to pardon her lover; he agrees on condition that the young man promise to desert the conspirators. Left alone the weary ruler drinks Paolo's potion and falls asleep. Gabriele, who has heard nothing, emerges from hiding and draws his knife, but Amelia returns in time to stop him from murdering her father. At last Gabriele learns the truth and implores the Doge's forgiveness. As cries of rebellion are heard, the two men rush off to help defend the palace.

ACT III. All Genoa celebrates Boccanegra's victory. Magnanimously he has set most of the rebel leaders free, including Fiesco, but the traitorous Paolo is condemned to death. On his way to execution the villain informs Fiesco that he has managed to poison the Doge. A Captain announces that revels must end in memory of the fallen heroes of the revolution. Boccanegra staggers in, gravely ill. Fiesco, still bent on revenge, reveals to the Doge his true identity, whereupon he learns who Amelia really is. Stunned, Fiesco tells Boccanegra that Paolo has poisoned him. As the Doge dies, he blesses the newly married Gabriele and Amelia, asking that the youth be proclaimed the new Doge. Fiesco announces Boccanegra's death to the people.

*Courtesy Opera News.*

# CAST OF CHARACTERS

### Prologue

SIMON BOCCANEGRA, a corsair in the service of the Genoese republic . Baritone

JACOPO FIESCO, a Genoese noble . . . . . . . . . . . . . Bass

PAOLO ALBIANI, a gold-spinner of Genoa . . . . . . . . . Bass

PIETRO, a commoner of Genoa . . . . . . . . . . . . Baritone

Sailors, populace, servants of Fiesco, etc.

### The Drama

SIMON BOCCANEGRA, first Doge of Genoa . . . . . . . . . Baritone

AMELIA GRIMALDI, actually Maria Boccanegra, daughter of Simon . . Soprano

JACOPO FIESCO, known as Andrea . . . . . . . . . . . . Bass

GABRIELE ADORNO, a Genoese gentleman . . . . . . . . . Tenor

PAOLO ALBIANI, favorite courtier of the Doge . . . . . . . . Bass

PIETRO, another courtier . . . . . . . . . . . . . Baritone

A CAPTAIN OF ARCHERS . . . . . . . . . . . . . . Tenor

AMELIA'S MAID . . . . . . . . . . . . . Mezzo-Soprano

Soldiers, sailors, populace, senators, the Doge's court, etc.

The action takes place in and near Genoa in the middle of the 14th Century. Twenty-five years pass between the prologue and the drama.

# SYNOPSIS OF SCENES

# SIMON BOCCANEGRA

## PROLOGO

### Una Piazza di Genova

*Nel fondo la chiesa di San Lorenzo. A destra il palazzo dei Fieschi, con gran balcone: nel muro, di fianco al balcone, è un'immagine, davanti a cui arde un lanternino; a sinistra altre case. Varie strade conducono alla piazza. É notte.*

PAOLO

Che dicesti? All'onor di primo abate
Lorenzin, l'usuriere?

PIETRO

Altro proponi di lui più degno!

PAOLO

Il prode, che dai nostri
Mari cacciava l'african pirata,
E al ligure vessillo
Rese l'antica rinomanza altera.

PIETRO

Intesi . . . e il premio?

PAOLO

Oro, possanza, onore.

PIETRO

Vendo a tal prezzo il popolar favore.
*(Si danno la mano; Pietro parte.)*

PAOLO

Abborriti, patrizî,
Alle cime ove alberga il vostro orgoglio,
Disprezzato plebeo, salire io voglio.

SIMONE *(entra frettoloso)*
Un amplesso . . . Che avvenne?
Da Savona perchè qui m'appellasti?

PAOLO

All'alba eletto
Esser vuoi nuovo abate?

SIMONE

Io? . . . No.

PAOLO

Ti tenta ducal corona?

SIMONE

Vaneggi?

PAOLO *(con intenzione)*
E Maria?

SIMONE

O vittima innocente
Del funesto amor mio! Dimmi, di lei
Che sai? Le favellasti?

PAOLO

*(additando il palazzo Fieschi)*
Prigioniera geme in quella magion.

SIMONE

Maria!

PAOLO

Negarla al Doge chi potria?

SIMONE

Misera!

PAOLO

Assenti?

SIMONE

Paolo . . .

PAOLO

Tutto disposi . . . e sol ti chiedo
Parte ai perigli e alla possanza.

SIMONE

Sia.

PAOLO

In vita ed in morte?

SIMONE

Sia.

PAOLO

S'appressa alcun . . . T'ascondi . . .
Per poco ancor, mistero ti circondi.

*(Simone s'allontana. Paolo si trae in disparte presso il palazzo dei Fieschi. Pietro, marinai e artigiani entrano.)*

PIETRO

All'alba tutti qui verrete?

1

# SIMON BOCCANEGRA

## PROLOGUE

### A square in Genoa

*The church of San Lorenzo is in the background. At the right stands the palace of the Fieschi with a wide balcony; in the adjoining wall a small light is seen burning in a shrine. At the left other houses line streets leading to the square. It is night.*

PAOLO

What did you say?
For the noble post of abbot
Lorenzin, money lender?

PIETRO

Is there a rival of equal stature?

PAOLO

The leader who has freed our ocean
From all the bands of evil pirates
Until our ancient banners
Once more may raise their heads in
    pride and glory.

PIETRO

But tell me . . . your offer?

PAOLO

Money, and power, and honor.

PIETRO

Such is the price I'll take to win the
    people.
*(They shake hands; Pietro leaves.)*

PAOLO

I despise you, patricians,
On the heights where your pride of
    place can seat you
As a man of the people I would meet
    you.

SIMONE *(entering hurriedly)*

I salute you . . . What's happened?
From Savona I have come as you called
    me.

PAOLO

At daybreak the people may choose you
    as abbot.

SIMONE

Abbot? No.

PAOLO

The dukedom, it does not tempt you?

SIMONE

You're raving?

PAOLO *(pointedly)*

And Maria?

SIMONE

O victim of my innocent, ill-fated devo-
    tion!
Tell me, you know her fate? You've
    spoken with her?

PAOLO

*(pointing to the Fieschi palace)*

In that palace she laments day and
    night.

SIMONE

Maria!

PAOLO

But from the Doge what man could
    keep her?

SIMONE

Wretched girl!

PAOLO

You'll take it?

SIMONE

Paolo . . .

PAOLO

Then all is settled . . .
And my reward is sharing the dangers
    coming with power.

SIMONE

Granted.

PAOLO

Both now and forever?

SIMONE

Granted.

PAOLO

Someone is near . . . Go hide you . . .
For just a day in mystery abide you.

*(Simone withdraws. Paolo steps back to another part of the Fieschi palace. Pietro comes in with a crowd of sailors and workmen.)*

PIETRO

At daybreak surely all are coming?

1

CORO

Tutti.

PIETRO

Niun pei patrizi?

CORO

Niuno. A Lorenzino
Tutti il voto darem.

PIETRO

Venduto è ai Fieschi.

CORO

Dunque chi fia l'eletto?

PIETRO

Un prode.

CORO

Sì.

PIETRO

Un popolan.

CORO

Ben dici . . . ma fra i nostri sai l'uom?

PIETRO

Sì.

CORO

E chi? Risuoni il nome suo.

PAOLO (avanzandosi)

Simone Boccanegra.

CORO

Simone; Il Corsaro!

PAOLO

Sì. Il Corsaro all'alto scranno.

CORO

È qui?

PAOLO

Verrà.

CORO

E i Fieschi?

PAOLO

Taceranno.

(Chiama tutti intorno a sè; quindi,
indicando il palazzo dei Fieschi, dice
loro con mistero.)

L'atra magion vedete? De' Fieschi è
    l'empio ostello,
Una beltà infelice geme sepolta in
    quello;
Sono i lamenti suoi la sola voce umana
Che risuonar s'ascolta nell'ampia tomba
    arcana.

CORO

Già volgono tre lune, che la gentil
    sembianza
Non rallegrò i veroni della romita
    stanza;
Passando ogni pietoso invan mirar desia
La bella prigioniera, la misera Maria.

PAOLO

Si schiudon quelle porte solo al patrizio
    altero,
Che ad arte si ravvolge nell'ombre del
    mistero . . .

CORO

È vero, è ver.

PAOLO

Ma vedi in notte cupa per le deserte
    sale
Errar sinistra vampa, qual d'anima
    infernale.

CORO

Par l'antro dei fantasimi! Oh, qual
    orror!

(Dal palazzo Fieschi si vede il
riverbero d'un lume.)

PAOLO

Guardate,
La feral vampa appare.

CORO

Oh ciel!

PAOLO

V'allontanate.
Si caccino i demonii col segno della
    croce all'alba.

CORO

Qui.

PAOLO

Simone.

CORO

Simone ad una voce.

(Partono.)

FIESCO (esce dal palazzo)

A te l'estremo addio, palagio altero,
Freddo sepolcro dell'angiolo mio!
Nè a proteggerti valsi! Oh maledetto!
Oh vile seduttore!

(volgendosi all'Immagine)

**CHORUS**

Surely.

**PIETRO**

Who's for the nobles?

**CHORUS**

No one.
To Lorenzin we all have promised our
vote.

**PIETRO**

He's sold to Fiesco.

**CHORUS**

Who then will be elected?

**PIETRO**

A leader.

**CHORUS**

Yes.

**PIETRO**

A common man . . .

**CHORUS**

Well spoken . . . is the man one of us?

**PIETRO**

Yes.

**CHORUS**

But who? You tell us what his name is!

PAOLO (*coming forward*)

Simone Boccanegra.

**CHORUS**

Simone! What, the corsair!

**PAOLO**

Yes, raise the corsair to the
dukedom . . .

**CHORUS**

He's here?

**PAOLO**

He'll come.

**CHORUS**

The Fieschi?

**PAOLO**

They'll be silent.

(*He gathers the men about him, pointing mysteriously to the palace.*)

Dark is that evil prison, home of the
Fiesco nobles.
Within its walls a woman sighs at her
secret troubles;
Only her lamentations echo through
walls so haunted,
Breaking the eerie silence, there where
man's pride is flaunted.

**CHORUS**

Full many a moon has passed since her
gentle presence only
Appeared at the balcony steps of her
room so sad and lonely.
And every kindly stranger in vain has
sought to see her.
The prisoner so lovely, the wretched
girl Maria.

**PAOLO**

Only one man may enter, all of the
rest forbidden,
Noble his rank and station, deep in the
shadows hidden.

**CHORUS**

How true. How true.

**PAOLO**

Through those deserted chambers,
bleak with a gloom nocturnal,
One may see lights that wander from
some abode infernal.

**CHORUS**

A phantom from some dark abode! O
dreadful sight!

**PAOLO**

(*pointing to a light in the palace*)

You see it! Sadly the flame is shining.

**CHORUS**

O God!

**PAOLO**

Let us be leaving.
The cross can curb the demon by all
its holy powers.
At daybreak.

**CHORUS**

Here.

**PAOLO**

Simone.

**CHORUS**

We all demand Simone.

(*They all depart.*)

**FIESCO**

(*emerging from the palace*)

A last farewell I bid you, my haughty
palace,
Tomb of my darling, the tomb of my
angel.
All my care was for nothing!
Curses upon him, the villainous
seducer!

(*turning toward the shrine*)

E tu, Vergin, soffristi
Rapita a lei la verginal corona?
Ah! Che dissi? Deliro! Ah, mi perdona!
Il lacerato spirito
Del mesto genitore
Era serbato a strazio
D'infamia e di dolore.

(*S'odono lamenti dall'
interno del palazzo.*)

DONNE

É morta! A lei s'apron le sfere!
Mai più non la vedremo in terra!

UOMINI

Miserere! Miserere!

FIESCO

Il serto a lei de' martiri
Pietoso il cielo diè . . .
Resa al fulgor degli angeli,
Prega, Maria, per me.

(*Varie persone escono dal palazzo, e
traversando mestamente la piazza
s'allontanano. Simone ritorna in
scena esultante.*)

SIMONE

Suona ogni labbro il mio nome.
O Maria! Forse in breve potrai
    dirmi tuo sposo!

(*Scorge Fiesco.*)

Alcun veggo! Chi fia?

FIESCO

Simone?

SIMONE

Tu?

FIESCO

Qual cieco fato a oltraggiarmi ti traea?
Sul tuo capo io qui chiedea
L'ira vindice del ciel.

SIMONE

Padre mio, pietà t'imploro
Supplichevole a' tuoi piedi!
Il perdono a me concedi!

FIESCO

Tardi è omai.

SIMONE

Non sii crudel.
Sublimarmi a lei sperai
Sovra l'ali della gloria,
Strappai serti alla vittoria
Per l'altare dell'amor.

FIESCO

Io fea plauso al tuo valore,
Ma le offese non perdono . . .
Te vedessi asceso al trono.

SIMONE

Taci!

FIESCO

Segno all'odio mio
E all'anátema di Dio
È di Fiesco l'offensor.

SIMONE

Pace . . .

FIESCO

No! Pace non fora
Se pria l'un di noi non mora.

SIMONE

Vuoi col sangue mio placarti?

(*Gli presenta il petto.*)

Qui ferisci . . .

FIESCO

(*ritirandosi con orgoglio*)

Assassinarti?

SIMONE

Sì, m'uccidi, e almen sepolta
Fia con me tant' ira.

FIESCO

Ascolta.
Se concedermi vorrai
L'innocente sventurata
Che nascea dimpuro amor,
Io, che ancor non la mirai,
Giuro renderla beata,
E tu avrai perdono allor.

SIMONE

Nol poss'io.

FIESCO

Perchè?

SIMONE

Rubella sorte lei rapì.

FIESCO

Favella.

SIMONE

Del mar sul lido fra gente ostile
Crescea nell'ombra quella gentile;
Crescea lontana dagli occhi miei,
Vegliava annosa donna su lei.
Di là una notte varcando, solo
Dalla mia nave scesi a quel' suolo.

And you, O blessed Virgin,
You could not safeguard her innocence
 and virtue?
Ah! What madness! Forgive me! I
 would not hurt you!
Love that has torn a father's heart
Sad, as the fates ordained it,
Was at the least preserved to him—
Dishonor has not stained it.

WOMEN
(*lamenting from within the palace*)
She's perished, and the heavens have
 opened,
We shall see her no more among us.

MEN
Miserere! Miserere!

FIESCO
A martyr's crown will grace her brow
As heaven hears my plea,
Raised to the skies on angel wings,
Pray, O my love, for me.
(*People emerge from the palace, cross-
ing the square sadly and withdraw-
ing. Simone returns, joyfully.*)

SIMONE
All the world cries for Simone.
O Maria, in a moment you may call
 me your husband!
(*He perceives Fiesco.*)
Here is someone. Who are you?

FIESCO
Simon?

SIMONE
You?

FIESCO
What is the fate that has brought you
 to offend me?
I have prayed that the Lord may send
 me
Angry vengeance on your head.

SIMONE
At your feet I would implore you,
Father, you alone can shield me,
And your pardon you can yield me . . .

FIESCO
It is late.

SIMONE
You do me wrong. I had hoped to rise
 to her
On the heights of glory winging,
With a wreath of triumph bringing
To the altar of our love.

FIESCO
I applaud your deeds of valor,
But my hands will never bless you.
On the throne I may address you . . .

SIMONE
Silence!

FIESCO
Hatred falls upon you
And the curse of heav'n is on you,
You who sullied Fiesco's name.

SIMONE
Pardon!

FIESCO
There's no replying
Till one of us two men is dying.

SIMONE
Will my blood with mercy fill you?
(*baring his breast*)
You may strike me.

FIESCO
(*haughtily turning away*)
I will not kill you.

SIMONE
Strike me, kill me, and then your anger
May be buried with me.

FIESCO
Now listen:
If you wish to sue for peace
That unhappy little daughter
Who betokens all of your lust.
If you promise to release her
Every comfort will be brought her,
I'll forgive you if I must.

SIMONE
Ah, I cannot.

FIESCO
And why?

SIMONE
The fates have stolen her away.

FIESCO
But tell me.

SIMONE
There among aliens in seaside meadows
Grew the small maiden, deep in the
 shadows.
Far from my keeping, steadily growing,
While an old woman nursed her,
 unknowing.
Sailing at night as my voyage ended,
There on that lonely shore I descended,

Corsi alla casa . . . n'era la porta
Serrata, muta!

FIESCO

La donna?

SIMONE

Morta!

FIESCO

E la tua figlia?

SIMONE

Misera, trista,
Tre giorni pianse, tre giorni errò.
Scomparve poscia, nè fu più vista,
D'allora indarno cercata io l'ho.

FIESCO

Se il mio desire compier non puoi,
Pace non puote esser fra noi!
Addio, Simone!

(Gli volge le spalle.)

SIMONE

Coll'amor mio saprò placarti.

FIESCO

(freddo, senza guardarlo)

No.

SIMONE

M'odi.

FIESCO

Addio.

(S'allontana, poi s'arresta in
disparte ad osservare.)

SIMONE

Oh, de' Fieschi implacata, orrida razza!
E tra cotesti rettili nascea
Quella pura beltà? Vederla io
  voglio . . .
Coraggio!

(Va alla porta del palazzo
e batte tre colpi.)

Muta è la magion de' Fieschi?
Dischiuse son le porte!
Quale mistero! Entriam.

(Entra nel palazzo.)

FIESCO

T'inoltra e stringi gelida salma.

SIMONE

(comparisce sul balcone)

Nessuno! Qui sempre
Silenzio e tenebra!

(Stacca il lanternino della Immagine
ed entra.)

Maria! Maria!

FIESCO

L'ora suonò del tuo castigo.

SIMONE

(esce dal palazzo, atterrito)

É sogno!
Sì; spaventoso, atroce sogno è il mio!

VOCI (da lontano)

Boccanegra!

SIMONE

Quai voci!

VOCI (più vicine)

Boccanegra!

SIMONE

Eco d'inferno è questo!

(Paolo, Pietro, marinai, popolo d'ambo
i sessi, con faci accese.)

PAOLO E PIETRO

Doge il popol t'acclama!

SIMONE

Via fantasmi! Via!

PAOLO E PIETRO

Che di' tu?

SIMONE

Paolo! Una tomba!

PAOLO

Un trono!

FIESCO (tra sè)

Doge Simon? M'arde l'inferno in petto!

CORO

Viva Simon, del popolo l'eletto!

(Le campane suonano a stormo.)

## ATTO PRIMO

### SCENA I

Giardino de' Grimaldi fuori di Genova
*Alla sinstra il palazzo; di fronte il mare.*
*Spunta l'aurora.*

AMELIA (guardando verso il mare)

Come in quest'ora bruna
Sorridon gli astri e il mare!
Come s'unisce, o luna,

Ran up to find her, her whom I cher-
ished.
The cottage—silent!

FIESCO

The woman?

SIMONE

Perished.

FIESCO

As for your daughter?

SIMONE

No one to guide her,
Three days she wandered, weeping
with pain.
Later she vanished, no one had spied
her,
Vainly I've sought her, sought her in
vain.

FIESCO

If my desire you may not fulfill,
Nothing between us follows but ill!
Farewell, Boccanegra!

(*He turns away.*)

SIMONE

With all my heart I shall try to win
you.

FIESCO

(*coldly, without looking at him*)
No.

SIMONE

Hatred.

FIESCO

Farewell, then.

(*He withdraws, but stands apart to
watch Simone.*)

SIMONE

Oh those Fieschi, implacable and
hateful!
And from the vipers they have bred
What beauty and virtue have come!
I wish to see her. Have courage.

(*He goes to the gates of the palace and
knocks three times.*)

Silence in the Fieschi palace?
The portals are unbolted!
What is the answer? I'll try.

(*He enters the palace.*)

FIESCO

Go in and find a corpse that is frozen.

SIMONE

(*appearing on the balcony*)
There's no one!
But silence and black obscurity!

(*Taking the lamp from the shrine, he
goes inside.*)
Maria! Maria!

FIESCO

This is the hour of retribution.

SIMONE

(*coming out, terrified*)
I'm dreaming! Yes, I'm frightened,
This is a dreadful nightmare!

VOICES (*in the distance*)

Boccanegra!

SIMONE

Those voices!

VOICES (*coming nearer*)

Boccanegra!

SIMONE

Echoes of hell, I hear you!

(*Paolo and Pietro hurry in with a
crowd of sailors and townsfolk,
carrying lighted torches.*)

PAOLO AND PIETRO

You are Doge by acclamation!

SIMONE

Leave me you phantoms, leave me!

PAOLO AND PIETRO

What is this?

SIMONE

Paolo! I have lost her.

PAOLO

You've triumphed.

FIESCO (*aside*)

Simon as Doge? Rage is on fire within
me!

CHORUS

Viva Simon, elected by the people!

(*The bells ring.*)


ACT ONE

Scene 1

The Grimaldi gardens, near Genoa.

*The palace at the left; opposite, the
sea. Day is breaking.*

AMELIA (*watching the sea*)

Lovely, when day is early,
Starlight the ocean blesses!
See how the moon, so pearly

All'onda il tuo chiaror!
Amante amplesso pare
Di due verginei cor!
Ma gli astri e la marina
Che dicono alla mente
Dell'orfana meschina?
La notte atra, crudel,
Quando la pia morente
Sclamò: Ti guardi il ciel.
O altero ostel, soggiorno
Di stirpe ancor più altera,
Il tetto disadorno
Non obliai per te!
Solo in tua pompa austera
Amor sorride a me.
S'inalba il ciel, ma l'amoroso canto
Non s'ode ancora!
Ei mi terge ogni dì, come l'aurora
La rugiada de fior, del ciglio il pianto.

GABRIELE (*ben lontana*)

Cielo di stelle orbato,
Di fior vedovo prato,
È l'alma senza amor.

AMELIA

Ciel! La sua voce! È desso!
Ei s'avvicina! Oh gioia!

GABRIELE (*più vicino*)

Se manca il cor che t'ama,
Non empiono tua brama
Oro, possanza, onor.

AMELIA

Ei vien! L'amor
M'avvampa in sen
E spezza il fren
L'ansante cor!

GABRIELE (*in scena*)

Anima mia!

AMELIA

Perchè sì tardi giungi?

GABRIELE

Perdona, o cara . . . I lunghi indugi
    miei
T'apprestano grandezza.

AMELIA

Pavento . . .

GABRIELE

Che?

AMELIA

L'arcano tuo conobbi . . .
A me sepolcro appresti,
Il patibolo a te!

GABRIELE

Che pensi?

AMELIA

Io amo
Andrea qual padre, il sai;
Pur m'atterisce! In cupa
Notte non vi mirai
Sotto le tetre volte errar sovente
Torbidi, irrequieti?

GABRIELE

Chi?

AMELIA

Tu, e Andrea,
E Lorenzino ed altri . . .

GABRIELE

Ah taci . . . il vento
Ai tiranni potria recar tai voci!
Parlan le mura . . . un delator s'asconde
Ad ogni passo.

AMELIA

Tu tremi?

GABRIELE

I funesti fantasmi scaccia!

AMELIA

Fantasmi dicesti?
Vieni a mirar la cerula
Marina tremolante;
Là Genova torreggia
Sul talamo spumante;
Là i tuoi nemici imperano,
Vincerli indarno speri . . .
Ripara i tuoi pensieri
Al porto dell'amor.

GABRIELE

Angiol che dall'empireo
Piegasti a terra l'ale,
E come faro sfolgori
Sul tramite mortale,
Non ricercar dell'odio
I funebri misteri;
Ripara i tuoi pensieri
Al porto dell'amor

AMELIA
(*fissando a destra*)

Ah!

GABRIELE

Che fia?

Gives radiance to the sea
Like lovers' fond caresses
In virgin purity!

But stars and waves are lying
If they profess a meaning
To one who was deserted
At nightfall, cruel and late,
By her who died when crying:
May heaven guard your fate!

For you, O noble setting
Of those whose rank is splendid,
I shall not be forgetting
All that I left behind.
My rapture is not ended,
For love is smiling, kind.

The sun appears, surely my love is
  sleeping,
I cannot hear him
Yet he comes every day. When I feel
  near him
As the sun dries the dew, he stills my
  weeping.

GABRIELE'S VOICE (*distant*)
Heaven that never lightens,
A meadow that never brightens,
Is one who knows no love.

AMELIA
God, it is his voice! He's coming!
He's coming nearer! Oh rapture!

GABRIELE'S VOICE (*nearer*)
If love alone be lacking
All pleasures will be slacking:
Power and gold and fame.

AMELIA
He comes to rouse my burning breast,
My heart is blessed,
I call his name! Ah!

GABRIELE (*entering*)
My own beloved!

AMELIA
But why are you so tardy?

GABRIELE
Forgive my dearest. The long delays
  that kept me
May fill your life with grandeur.

AMELIA
I fear it . . .

GABRIELE
What?

AMELIA
For I have learned your secret . . .
For me a tomb is waiting,
But the gallows for you.

GABRIELE
You think so?

AMELIA
I love him like a father—Andrea—
And yet I fear him, for in the night I've
  seen them wander
Beneath the gloomy portals, oh, so
  often,
Restlessly apathetic.

GABRIELE
Who?

AMELIA
You, and Andrea, and Lorenzin and
  others . . .

GABRIELE
Be careful . . . the wind can repeat what
  we whisper
To the tyrants. Even the walls speak.
A spy may be in hiding at every
  footstep.

AMELIA
You tremble?

GABRIELE
Drive away all these morbid fancies!

AMELIA
They're fancies, you tell me?
Look at the waves of azure hue,
Tremulous like the ocean;
Genoa seems to tower
Above their gentle motion.
There rule your deadly enemies,
Vainly you hope to quell them . . .
Thoughts such as these—come, dispel
  them
And talk to me of love.

GABRIELE
Angel, flying from heavenly heights
With folded wings to bless me,
How can you blaze my earthly trail,
With gentleness caress me?
Do not seek out to know their ways,
Out of your mind expel them
Thoughts such as these, dispel them,
And talk to me of love.

AMELIA (*staring at the right*)
Ah!

GABRIELE
What is it?

AMELIA
Vedi là quell'uom? Qual ombra
Ogni dì appar.

GABRIELE
Forse un rival?

ANCELLA (entra)
Del Doge un messaggier di te chiede.

AMELIA
S'appressi.
(L'Ancella parte.)

GABRIELE (va per uscire)
Chi sia veder vogl'io . . .

AMELIA (fermandolo)
T'arresta.

PIETRO
(inchinandosi ad Amelia)
Il Doge dalle caccie tornando di
Savona
Questa magion visitar brama.

AMELIA
Il puote.
(Pietro parte.)

GABRIELE
Il Doge qui?

AMELIA
Mia destra a chieder viene.

GABRIELE
Per chi?

AMELIA
Pel favorito suo. D'Andrea
Vola in cerca . . . Affrettati . . . va . . .
prepara
Il rito nuzial . . . mi guida all'ara.

AMELIA E GABRIELE
Sì, sì dell'ara il giubilo
Contrasti il fato avverso,
E tutto l'universo
Io sfiderò con te.
Innamorato anelito
É del destin più forte;
Amanti oltre la morte
Sempre vivrai con me.
(Amelia entra in palazzo. Gabriele va
per uscire dalla destra e incontra
Andrea.)

GABRIELE (da sè)
Propizio ei giunge!

ANDREA
Tu sì mattutino qui?

GABRIELE
A dirti . . .

ANDREA
Ch' ami Amelia.

GABRIELE
Tu che lei vegli con paterna cura
A nostre nozze assenti?

ANDREA
Alto mistero sulla vergine incombe.

GABRIELE
E qual?

ANDREA
Se parlo, forse tu più non l'amerai.

GABRIELE
Non teme ombra d'arcani l'amor mio!
T'ascolto!

ANDREA
Amelia tua d'umile stirpe nacque.

GABRIELE
La figlia dei Grimaldi?

ANDREA
No . . . la figlia
Dei Grimaldi morì tra consacrate
Vergini in Pisa. Un'orfana raccolta
Nel chiostro il dì che fu d'Amelia
estremo
Ereditò sua cella.

GABRIELE
Ma come dei Grimaldi
Anco il nome prendea?

ANDREA
De' fuorusciti
Perseguia le ricchezze il nuovo Doge;
E la mentita Amelia alla rapace
Man sottrarle potea.

GABRIELE
L'orfana adoro.

ANDREA
Di lei sei degno!

GABRIELE
A me fia dunque unita?

AMELIA

Do you see that man? That shadow
Comes near each day.

GABRIELE

A rival love?

SERVANT (*entering*)

The Doge has sent a man with a
  message.

AMELIA

Go call him.
    (*The servant leaves.*)

GABRIELE (*turning to go out*)

I'll see who is waiting.

AMELIA (*holding him back*)

One moment!

PIETRO

(*entering and bowing to Amelia*)

Our master is returning from hunting
  at Savona
And he desires to make a visit.

AMELIA

He's welcome.
    (*Pietro departs.*)

GABRIELE

The Doge is here?

AMELIA

He comes with a proposal.

GABRIELE

For whom?

AMELIA

For his beloved courtier.
Go hasten to find Andrea . . . and lose
  no time . . .
Go, our wedding must be prepared, we
  must be married.

AMELIA AND GABRIELE

Ah yes, our plighted happiness
Will shield us from disaster,
No other earthly master
I shall accept but you.
Love that is true and passionate
Than any fate is stronger,
And life shall last no longer
Than I shall live for you.
(*Amelia enters the palace. Gabriele,
  about to depart, meets Andrea.*)

GABRIELE (*to himself*)

A timely visit!

ANDREA

You! How early you are here!

GABRIELE

To tell you—

ANDREA

Yes, Amelia.

GABRIELE

You who have loved her with a father's
  interest,
You will permit our marriage?

ANDREA

There is a secret hanging over Amelia.

GABRIELE

But what?

ANDREA

Did you know, perhaps your love would
  quickly fade?

GABRIELE

A love like mine does not shrink from
  any secrets.
So tell me.

ANDREA

Amelia's parentage was very humble.

GABRIELE

The child of the Grimaldis?

ANDREA

The child of the Grimaldis, she perished in a convent
With the nuns, in Pisa. A foundling
  child was rescued
The very same day that poor Amelia
  left us
And took the empty lodging.

GABRIELE

But how did the Grimaldis
Give their name to the orphan?

ANDREA

All of the riches any exile possessed
  were confiscated.
Amelia, as an heiress, alone could stop
  the Doge from taking their gold.

GABRIELE

I love the orphan.

ANDREA

And you are worthy!

GABRIELE

Then you will bless our marriage?

ANDREA

On earth and in heaven!

GABRIELE

You give me courage!

ANDREA

Come to me that I may bless you
In the peace that fills this hour.
May your life be rich in power
Which your love and your country
   impart.

GABRIELE

Ancient echoes seem to possess you
While your dear voice sounds a holy
   spell.
Saintly memories, I tell you,
Will inspire this faithful heart.
   (*flourish of trumpets*)
Here is the Doge. Away! He must not
find you.

ANDREA

Ah! Your avenger soon will stand behind you.
   (*They leave.*)

DOGE

(*entering, with Paolo and hunting
party*)
Paolo.

PAOLO

My lord!

DOGE

A crisis has arisen which causes us to
leave.

PAOLO

When, sir?

DOGE

When the hour has sounded.

PAOLO (*noticing Amelia*)

Ah, she is fair!
(*He leaves, following the Doge's
retinue.*)

DOGE

Am I addressing Amelia Grimaldi?

AMELIA

That is the name they call me.

DOGE

Is it not true your exiled brothers
Desire to behold their country?

AMELIA

They do, sir, but . . .

DOGE

I know it . . .
They will not yield to me, these haughty
   brothers,
And thus to meet their pride as Doge,
   I answer . . .
   (*He hands her a paper.*)

AMELIA (*reading the paper*)

A pardon? You will forgive them?

DOGE

It is to you they owe my gift of mercy.
Tell me, within this lonely spot,
Why is your beauty hidden?
Do you not mourn the worldly joys,
The lights that are forbidden?
I see a blush awaken . . .

AMELIA

I'm happy. You are mistaken.

DOGE

But love—all maidens need it.

AMELIA

Ah, my heart, you seem to read it!
I love a good devoted man
Whose heart is warm and sunny . . .
But there's a villain at my door
Yearns for Grimaldi money.

DOGE

Paolo!

AMELIA

You've named the rascal.
Since you are seeing
So kindly to my life and future welfare,
I will tell you the secret of my being.
I am not a Grimaldi.

DOGE

My God! Then who?

AMELIA

As an orphan I lived in poverty
Under the care of a kindly old peasant.
It was close to the shore so pleasant,
Near to Pisa.

DOGE

In Pisa—you?

AMELIA

She was old in years and feeble,
But she fed me, gathered the fuel;
Yet the heavens were very cruel,
Ah! She was taken, she left me too.
She bestowed on me a picture
With her cold and trembling fingers,
How the likeness quietly lingers

ANDREA
In terra e in ciel!

GABRIELE
Ah! tu mi dai la vita!

ANDREA
Vieni a me, ti benedico
Nella pace di quest'ora,
Lieto vivi e fido adora
L'angiol tuo, la patria, il ciel!

GABRIELE
Eco pia del tempo antico.
La tua voce è un casto incanto.
Serberà ricordo santo
Di quest' ora il cor fedel.
(squilli di trombe)
Ie Doge vien. Partiam. Ch'ei non ti
scorga.

ANDREA
Ah! presto il dì della vendetta sorga!
(Partono. Doge, Paolo e seguito.)

DOGE
Paolo!

PAOLO
Signor!

DOGE
Ci spronano gli eventi,
Di qua partir convien.

PAOLO
Quando?

DOGE
Allo squillo dell'ora.

PAOLO (guardando Amelia)
Oh qual beltà!
(Parte col séguito.)

DOGE
Favella il Doge ad Amelia Grimaldi?

AMELIA
Così nomata io sono.

DOGE
E gli esuli fratelli tuoi non punge
Desio di patria?

AMELIA
Possente . . . ma . . .

DOGE
Intendo.
A me inchinarsi sdegnano i
Grimaldi . . .
Così risponde a tanto orgoglio il
Doge . . .
(Le porge un foglio.)

AMELIA
Che veggio! Il lor perdono?

DOGE
E denno a te della clemenza il dono.
Dinne, perchè in quest'eremo
Tanta beltà chiudesti?
Del mondo mai le fulgide
Lusinghe non piangesti?
Il tuo rossor mel dice . . .

AMELIA
T'inganni! Io son felice.

DOGE
Agli anni tuoi l'amore.

AMELIA
Ah mi leggesti in core!
Amo uno spirto angelico
Che ardente mi riama . . .
Ma di me acceso, un perfido,
L'ôr de' Grimaldi brama.

DOGE
Paolo!

AMELIA
Quel vil nomasti! E poichè tanta
Pietà ti muove dei destini miei,
Vo' svelarti il segreto che mi ammanta.
Non sono una Grimaldi!

DOGE
Oh ciel! Chi sei?

AMELIA
Orfanella il tetto umile
M'accogliea d'una meschina,
Dove presso alla marina
Sorge Pisa.

DOGE
In Pisa tu?

AMELIA
Grave d'anni quella pia
Era solo a me sostegno;
Io provai del ciel lo sdegno,
Involata ella mi fu.
Colla tremola sua mano
Pinta effige mi porgea.
Le sembianze esser dicea

Della madre ignota a me.
Mi baciò, mi benedisse,
Levò al ciel, pregando, i rai . . .
Quante volte la chiamai,
L'eco sol risposta die'.

DOGE (*da sè*)

Se la speme, o ciel clemente,
Ch'or sorride all'alma mia,
Fosse sogno! . . . estinto io sia
Della larva al disparir!

AMELIA

Come tetro a me dolente
S'appressava l'avvenir!

DOGE

Dinne . . . alcun là non vedesti?

AMELIA

Uom di mar noi visitava . . .

DOGE

E Giovanna si nomava
Lei che i fati a te rapîr?

AMELIA

Sì.

DOGE

E l'effigie non somiglia questa?
(*Trae dal seno un ritratto, lo porge
ad Amelia, che fa altrettanto.*)

AMELIA

Uguali son!

DOGE

Maria!

AMELIA

Il nome mio!

DOGE

Sei mia figlia.

AMELIA

Io?

DOGE

M'abbraccia, o figlia mia.

AMELIA

Padre!
Stringi al   sen Maria che t'ama.

DOGE

Figlia, figlia, il cor ti chiama.
Figlia! a tal nome io palpito
Qual se m'aprisse i cieli.
Un mondo d' ineffabili
Letizie a me riveli;

Un paradiso il tenero
Padre ti schiuderà.
Di mia corona il raggio
La gloria tua sarà.

AMELIA

Padre! vedrai la vigile
Figlia a te sempre accanto;
Nell'ora melanconica
Asciugherò il tuo pianto.
Avrem gioie romite
Soltanto note al ciel,
Io la colomba mite
Sarò del regio ostel.
(*Amelia, accompagnata dal padre fino
alla soglia, entra nel palazzo.*)

PAOLO (*entra rapidamente*)

Che rispose?

DOGE

Rinunzia ogni speranza.

PAOLO

Doge, nol posso!

DOGE

Il voglio.
(*Entra nelle stanze d'Amelia.*)

PAOLO

Il vuoi! scordasti che mi devi il soglio?

PIETRO

Che disse?

PAOLO

A me negolla.

PIETRO

Che pensi tu?

PAOLO

Rapirla.

PIETRO

Come?

PAOLO

Sul lido a sera
La troverai solinga . . .
Sì tragga al mio naviglio;
Di Lorenzin si rechi alla magion.

PIETRO

S'ei nega?

PAOLO

Digli che so sue trame,
E presterammi aita . . .
Tu gran mercede avrai.

To the mother I knew was dead.
Then she kissed me and she blessed me,
Praying heaven not to take her,
Many times I tried to wake her,
Only echoes came instead.

DOGE (*to himself*)
Ah! If the hope, O merciful Heaven,
Smiling with joy on all that I cherish,
Prove a dream, ah, then let me perish,
As the phantom melts away.

AMELIA
Ah, how gloomily and sadly loomed the
　future every day!

DOGE
Tell me, you saw no human being?

AMELIA
Once a sailor came to see us.

DOGE
Was the woman's name Giovanna who
　was taken from your side?

AMELIA
Yes.

DOGE
(*taking a picture from his bosom and
　showing it to Amelia*)
And the miniature, was it like this one?

AMELIA
(*comparing it to her picture*)
The very same!

DOGE
Maria!

AMELIA
Yes, that is my name!

DOGE
You're my daughter.

AMELIA
I am?

DOGE
Embrace me, dearest daughter.

AMELIA
Father! Ah, hold me close, Maria calls
　you.

DOGE
Ah, mine, no matter what befalls you!
Daughter! The very name I say
Opens the heavens to me,
Opens a world of utter bliss
Shining with glory through me.

Gently we'll go to paradise
And open wide the doors.
Crowning my throne with glory,
This glory will be yours.

AMELIA
Father, a guardian at your side
I shall remain unsleeping;
And if the times are sorrowful
I will allay your weeping.
Alone we'll taste of pleasure,
Observed by heav'n above.
To guard the royal treasure
I'll be your gentle dove.
(*They embrace and the Doge leads her
　to the palace.*)

PAOLO (*entering rapidly*)
Will she have me?

DOGE
You cannot hope to win her.

PAOLO
My Lord, I will hope.

DOGE
My orders.
(*follows Amelia to her rooms*)

PAOLO
Your wish! Your will!
Have you forgotten what you owe me?

PIETRO
The verdict?

PAOLO
He will not yield her.

PIETRO
What is your plan?

PAOLO
To steal her.

PIETRO
Steal her?

PAOLO
She walks at evening alone beside the
　ocean.
You'll take her to my vessel
And hurry to the palace of Lorenzin.

PIETRO
He'll take us?

PAOLO
You'll tell him I know, know all his
　plots,
He won't be long deciding.
You, you'll have a rich reward.

PIETRO
Ella sarà rapita.

(*Escono.*)

SCENA 2

Sala del Consiglio nel Palazzo degli Abati.

(*Il Doge seduto sul seggio ducale; da un lato, dodici Consiglieri nobili; dall'altro lato, dodici Cinsiglieri popolani. Seduti a parte, quattro Consoli del Mare e i Connestabili. Paolo e Pietro stanno sugli ultimi seggi dei popolani. Un Araldo.*)

DOGE

Messeri, il re di Tartaria vi porge
Pegni di pace e ricchi doni e annunzia
Schiuso l'Eusin alle liguri prore.
Acconsentite?

TUTTI
Sì.

DOGE

Ma d'altro voto
Più generoso io vi richiedo.

ALCUNI
Parla.

DOGE

La stessa voce che tuonò su Rienzi,
Vaticinio di gloria e poi di morte,
Or su Genova tuona.

(*mostrando uno scritto*)

Ecco un messaggio del romito di Sorga,
    ei per Venezia
Supplica pace . . .

PAOLO (*interrompendolo*)

Attenda alle sue rime
Il cantor della bionda Avignonese.

TUTTI (*ferocemente*)
Guerra a Venezia!

DOGE

E con quest'urlo atroce
Fra due liti d'Italia erge Caino
La sua clava cruenta! Adria e Liguria
Hanno patria comune.

TUTTI
È nostra patria Genova.

(*tumulto lontano*)

PIETRO
Qual clamor!

ALCUNI
D'onde tai grida?

PAOLO

(*balzando al verone*)
Dalla piazza dei Fieschi.

TUTTI (*alzandosi*)
Una sommossa!

PAOLO

(*sempre alla finestra, lo ha raggiunto Pietro*)
Ecco una turba di fuggenti.

DOGE
Ascolta.

(*Il tumulto si fa più forte.*)

PAOLO
Si sperdon le parole.

VOCE INTERNE
Morte! Morte!

PAOLO (*a Pietro*)
È lui?

DOGE
Chi?

PIETRO
Guarda!

DOGE (*guardando*)

Ciel! Gabriele Adorno
Dalla plebe inseguito! Accanto ad esso
Combatte un Guelfo. A me un araldo.

PIETRO (*sommesso*)
Paolo, fuggi o sei côlto.

DOGE

(*guardando Paolo che s'avvia*)
Consoli del mare,
Custodite le soglie! Olà, chi fugge
È un traditor.

(*Paolo confuso s'arresta.*)

VOCI (*in piazza*)
Morte ai patrizi!

CONSIGLIERI NOBILI

(*sguainando le spade*)
All'armi!

PIETRO

That girl, I'll keep her well in hiding.
(*They depart.*)


Scene 2

The council chamber

(*The Doge is seated on the ducal
throne; on one side are twelve patrician councillors, on the other
twelve commoners. Seated apart are
four naval consuls and constables.
Paolo and Pietro stand in the last
ranks of the commoners. A herald is
in attendance.*)

DOGE

Your lordships, from Tartary the king
  has offered tokens of peace and rich
  donations,
Declares the Eusinian sea open now to
  our shipping.
Do you approve it?

ALL

Yes.

DOGE

But now I ask much more in the vote
  that you will give me.

ALL

Tell us!

DOGE

The very voice that thundered on
  Rienzi with a forecast of glory and
  then destruction, thunders now on
  our city.
(*showing a document*)
Here is a message from the hermit of
  Sorga; he asks of us a treaty with
  Venice.

PAOLO (*interrupting*)

Oh give him as an answer a poem to
  some Avignon beauty!

ALL (*fiercely*)

War now with Venice!

DOGE

And through this wicked shouting
With the quarrels of brothers, Cain is
  arising
And his cudgel is bloody.
Venice and Genoa are brotherly
  countries.

ALL

For us one country—Genoa!
(*distant tumult*)

PIETRO

What a noise!
(*runs to the balcony*)

COUNCILLORS

Where does it come from?

PAOLO

From the square of the Fieschi.

COUNCILLORS (*rising*)

It is a riot!

PAOLO (*with Pietro on the balcony*)

Listen . . . I can hear the rabble coming.

DOGE

I hear them.
(*The tumult grows louder.*)

PAOLO (*listening*)

But what is it they're saying?

VOICES

Kill him! Kill him!

PAOLO (*to Pietro*)

It's he!

DOGE

Who?

PIETRO

See him!

DOGE (*watching*)

Heavens! It's Gabriel Adorno, chased
  by the rabble!
And there's a Guelph who is close
  beside him.
Now send me a herald.

PIETRO (*excitedly*)

Paolo, flee or be taken.

DOGE (*watching the fleeing Paolo*)

Consuls of the navy, you will guard
  every portal!
Stop there! A traitor tries to flee.
(*Paolo, confused, stops short.*)

VOICES (*from the square*)

Kill all the nobles!

COUNCILLORS

(*unsheathing their swords*)
We'll fight them!

VOCI (*in piazza*)
Viva il popolo!

CONSIGLIERI POPOLARI

(*sguainando le spade*)
Evviva!

DOGE
E che? Voi pure?
Voi, qui, vi provocate?

VOCI (*in piazza*)
Morte al Doge!

DOGE
(*con fierezza*)
Morte al Doge? Sta ben.
(*Sarà giunto l'araldo.*)
Tu, araldo, schiudi
Le porte del palagio e annuncia al
    volgo
Gentilesco e plebeo ch'io non lo temo,
Che le minacci udii, che qui li
    attendo . . .
(*ai Consiglieri che ubbidiscono*)
Nelle guaine i brandi!

VOCI (*in piazza*)
Armi! Saccheggio!
Fuoco alle case!

ALTRE VOCI
Ai trabocchi!

ALTRE
Alla gogna!

DOGE
Squilla la tromba dell'araldo . . .ei
    parla!
Tutto è silenzio.

VOCI
Evviva il Doge!

DOGE
Ecco le plebi!
(*Irrompe la folla dei popolani, i Consiglieri, molte donne, alcuni fanciulli.
I Consiglieri nobili sempre divisi dai
popolani. Adorno e Fiesco afferrati
dal popolo.*)

POPOLO
Vendetta! Vendetta!
Spargasi il sangue del fiero uccisor!

DOGE (*ironicamente*)
Questa è dunque del popolo la voce?
Da lungi tuono d'uragan, da presso
Grido di donne e di fanciulli. Adorno,
Perchè impugni l'acciar?

GABRIELE
Ho trucidato Lorenzino.

POPOLO
Assassin!

GABRIELE
Ei la Grimaldi avea rapita.

DOGE (*tra sè*)
Orror!

POPOLO
Menti!

GABRIELE
Quel vile
Pria di morir disse che un uom possente
Al crimine l'ha spinto.

PIETRO (*a Paolo*)
Ah! sei scoperto!

DOGE (*con agitazione*)
E il nome suo?

GABRIELE
(*fissando il Doge con
tremenda ironia*)
T'acqueta! Il reo si spense
Pria di svelarlo.

DOGE
Che vuoi dir?

GABRIELE
(*terribilmente*)
Pel cielo!
Uom possente sei tu!

DOGE (*a Gabriele*)
Ribaldo!

GABRIELE
(*al Doge slanciandosi*)
Audace rapitor di fanciulle!

ALCUNI
Si disarmi!

GABRIELE
Empio corsaro incoronato! Muori!
(*Divincolandosi corre per ferire il
Doge.*)

VOICES (*from the square*)
Hail the people's cause!

PLEBEIAN COUNCILLORS
(*unsheathing their swords*)
The people!

DOGE
What now? You also?
You here, you would arouse them!

VOICES (*from the square*)
Death to Simon!

DOGE (*proudly*)
Death to Simon? Amen.
(*to the herald who has entered*)
You, herald, open the gates through all
the palace
And tell both gentlemen and people to
come,
I do not fear them. All of their threats
I've heard.
Here I await them. Now you may
sheathe your weapons.
(*The councillors obey.*)

VOICES (*from the square*)
Murder and pillage! Burn all the
houses!

OTHER VOICES
It's an ambush!

OTHERS
To the scaffold!

DOGE
Listen! The trumpet of the herald . . .
The message. Now all is silence.

VOICES
We hail him! Our Doge is Simon!

DOGE
Here come the people!
(*A crowd of townsfolk, women, children and councillors bursts into the
chamber. The patrician councillors
keep their distance from the commoners. Adorno and Fiesco are
brought in by the mob.*)

MOB
We're crying for vengeance, avenging a
murder!
Blood must be avenging the crime on
his head!

DOGE (*ironically*)
Can it be that I hear the people cry-
ing?
A tempest roaring from afar, and near
us
Crying of women and little children.
Adorno, are you grasping your sword?

GABRIELE
I've killed the wretched Lorenzino.

MOB
He is killed.

GABRIELE
Because he carried off Amelia.

DOGE (*to himself*)
Oh, no!

MOB
Liar!

GABRIELE
He told me before he died someone
of mighty power
Had driven him to action.

PIETRO (*to Paolo*)
Ah! You're discovered.

DOGE (*in agitation*)
What was his name?

GABRIELE
(*staring at the Doge with great irony*)
Don't worry! The wretch was silent.
He did not tell me.

DOGE
And you mean?

GABRIELE (*with terrifying menace*)
By heaven, you're the man who's
in power!

DOGE (*to Gabriele*)
You scoundrel!

GABRIELE (*rushing at the Doge*)
Abductor of young girls, you are
shameless!

COUNCILLORS
We'll disarm him.

GABRIELE
(*tearing himself free and rushing
to strike the Doge*)
Pirate, who rules our land with evil,
Die now!

AMELIA

(interponendosi fra i due assalitori e
il Doge)

Ferisci?

DOGE, FIESCO, GABRIELE

Amelia!

TUTTI

Amelia!

AMELIA

O Doge! Ah! Salva.
Salva l'Adorno tu.

DOGE

(alle guardie che si sono impossessate
di Gabriele per disarmarlo)

Nessun l'offenda.
Cade l'orgoglio e al suon del suo dolore
Tutta l'anima mia parla d'amore . . .
Amelia, di' come fosti rapita
E come al periglio potesti scampar.

AMELIA

Nell'ora soave che all'estasi invita
Soletta men givo sul lido del mar.
Mi cingon tre sgherri, m'accoglie un
    naviglio.
Soffocati non valsero i gridi . . .
Io svenni e al novello dischiuder del
    ciglio
Lorenzo in sue stanze presente mi
    vidi . . .

TUTTI

Lorenzo!

AMELIA

Mi vidi prigion dell'infame!
Io ben di quell'alma sapea la viltà.
Al Doge gli dissi, fien note tue trame,
Se a me sull'istante non dai libertà.
Confuso di tema, mi schiuse le
    porte . . .
Salvarmi l'audace minaccia potea.

TUTTI

Ei ben meritava, quell'empio, la morte.

AMELIA

V'è un più nefando che illeso ancor sta.

TUTTI

Chi dunque?

AMELIA

(fissando Paolo che sta dietro
    un gruppo di persone)

Ei m'ascolta . . . discerno le smorte
Sue labbra.

DOGE E GABRIELE

Chi dunque?

POPOLANI (minaccioso)

Un patrizio.

NOBILI (minaccioso)

Un plebeo.

POPOLANI (ai Nobili)

Abbasso le spade!

AMELIA

Terribili gridi!

NOBILI (ai Popolani)

Abbasso le scuri!

AMELIA

Pietà!

DOGE (possentemente)

Fratricidi!
Plebe! Patrizi! Popolo
Dalla feroce storia!
Erede sol dell'odio
Dei Spinola, dei Doria,
Mentre v'invita estatico
Il regno ampio dei mari,
Voi nei fraterni lari
Vi lacerate il cor.
Piango su voi, sul placido
Raggio del vostro clivo,
Là dove invan germoglia
Il ramo dell'ulivo.
Piango sulla mendace
Festa dei vostri fior,
E vo gridano: pace!
E vo gridano: amor!

AMELIA (a Fiesco)

Pace! lo sdegno immenso
Nascondi per pietà!
Pace! t'ispiri un senso
Di patria carità.

PIETRO (a Paolo)

Tutto fallì, la fuga
Sia tua salvezza almen!

AMELIA

(*entering and throwing herself between the Doge and his assailant*)

Strike me, then!

GABRIELE, DOGE AND FIESCO

Amelia!

COUNCILLORS AND PEOPLE

Amelia!

AMELIA

O Simon! Ah, save him . . . Let my Adorno live!

DOGE

(*to the guards who have arrested Gabriele to disarm him*)

Let no one hurt him!
Pride is forgotten; I see the tear-drops glisten
As she speaks of her love and I must listen . . . .
Amelia, tell us how you were abducted
And how you escaped from the arms of the man.

AMELIA

At evening near sunset, its beauty was soothing,
I walked by myself at the edge of the sea.
Three men fell upon me, and hastily turning
To a vessel, they stifled my crying.
I fainted—when I opened my eyes they were burning.
Lorenzo was standing and eagerly eyeing . . .

ALL

Lorenzo!

AMELIA

His prisoner there. His prisoner, shame to behold it!
How well did I know all that cowardly heart.
This outrage, I told him,
The Doge will be told it
If now at this instant these doors do not part.
He opened the portals; anxieties fill him,
And thus my defiance was able to save me.

ALL

Indeed it was proper that someone should kill him.

AMELIA

But there is another, another more wicked, who still is at large.

ALL

Who is he?

AMELIA

(*staring at Paolo in the background*)

He can hear me. His lips have already turned pallid.

DOGE AND GABRIELE

Who is he?

COMMONERS (*threateningly*)

A patrician.

NOBLES (*equally defiant*)

A plebeian.

COMMONERS (*to the nobles*)

Then down with your daggers!

AMELIA

What horrible clamor!

NOBLES (*to the commoners*)

Then down with your axes!

AMELIA

Oh help!

DOGE (*powerfully*)

Kill your brothers!
Townsfolk! Patricians!
All of you, sons of a fierce tradition,
And heirs of Dorian hatred for Spinola's ambition,
While all about, enchanting you,
Your wide realm is the ocean.
Gone is your fine emotion
And brothers wish to fight.
I weep for you, I weep to see the hillsides in bright illusion,
There where in vain the olive trees grow in rich profusion.
I weep—even the flowers lie unless the spirit move.
Yes, it is peace I ask for, and I appeal for love.

AMELIA (*to Fiesco*)

Quiet your mighty anger,
I beg you to be still.
Quiet! And hush your clangor
For Genoa's goodwill.

PIETRO (*to Paolo*)

Now flight alone can answer
Your need, for hope is gone.

PAOLO (*a Pietro*)
No, l'angue che mi fruga
È gonfio di velen!

GABRIELE (*da sè*)
Amelia è salva, e m'ama!
Sia ringraziato il ciel!
Disdegna ogni altra brama
L'animo mio fedel!

FIESCO (*tra sè*)
O patria! a qual mi serba
Vergogna il mio sperar!
Sta la città superba
Nel pugno d'un corsar!

CORO
(*fissando il Doge*)
Il suo commosso accento
Sa l'ira in noi calmar;
Vol di soave vento
Che rasserena il mar!

GABRIELE
(*offendo la spada al Doge*)
Ecco la spada.

DOGE
Questa notte prigione sarai, finchè la
     trama
Tutta si scopra. No, l'altera lama
Serba, non voglio che la tua parola.

GABRIELE
E sia!

DOGE
(*con forza terribile*)
Paolo!

PAOLO
(*sbucando dalla folla allibito*)
Mio duce!

DOGE
(*con tremenda maestà e con violenza
     sempre più formidabile*)
In te risiede
L'austero dritto popolar. E accolto
L'onore cittadin nella tua fede:
Bramo l'ausilio tuo . . . V'è in queste
     mura
Un vil che m'ode, e impallidisce in
     volto;
Già la mia man l' afferra per le
     chiome.
Io so il suo nome . . .
È nella sua paura.
Tu al cospetto del ciel e al mio cospetto
Sei testimon. Sul manigoldo impuro

Piombi il tuon del mio detto.
*Sia maledetto!*
          (*con immensa forza*)
E tu ripeti il giuro.

PAOLO
(*atterrito e tremante*)
*Sia maledetto!*
          (*da sè*)
Orror!

TUTTI
*Sia maledetto!*

## ATTO SECONDO
### Stanza del Doge
### nel Palazzo Ducale in Genova

*Porte laterali. Da un poggiolo si vede
la città. Un tavolo; un'anfora e una
tazza. Annotta.*

PAOLO
(*a Pietro traendolo verso
     il poggiolo*)
Quei due vedesti?

PIETRO
Sì.

PAOLO
Li traggi tosto
Dal carcer loro per l'andito ascoso,
Che questa chiave schiuderà.

PIETRO
T'intesi.
          (*Esce.*)

PAOLO
Me stesso ho maledetto!
E l'anátema
M'insegue ancor . . . e l'aura ancor ne
     trema!
Vilipeso . . . reietto
Dal Senato, da Genova, qui vibro
L'ultimo stral pria di fuggir; qui libro
La sorte tua, Doge, in quest'ansia
     estrema.
Tu, che m'offendi e che mi devi il
     trono,
Qui t'abbandono
Al tuo destino
In questa ora fatale.

(*Estrae un'ampolla, ne vuota
     il contenuto nella tazza.*)

Qui ti stillo una lenta, atra agonia . . .

PAOLO (*to Pietro*)
A serpent like a cancer
Drips poison flesh and bone.

GABRIELE
Amelia's safe, she loves me,
To heav'n I'll offer praise,
No other longing moves me,
With her I'll end my days.

FIESCO
What bitter shame, my city,
Without a hope, it's standing.
Proud was its name; oh pity
It fell to pirate hands.

CHORUS (*addressing the Doge*)
He calms us as he pleases,
How moving is his plea,
A breath of gentle breezes
To still the restless sea.

GABRIELE
(*offering his sword to the Doge*)
Here is my weapon.

DOGE
For the night you remain in our hands
Until the plot is fully uncovered.
No, take back the sword you offer,
I only ask your word of honor.

GABRIELE
I swear.

DOGE (*with terrific force*)
Paolo!

PAOLO
(*emerging in confusion
from the crowd*)
My master!

DOGE
(*majestically and with
growing violence*)
In you are vested the people's
honorable rights,
The honor of the citizens resides in
your credit;
I need your loyal aid.
Within this chamber there stands a
villain,
With pallid face he listens,
I feel my hand upon his head already.
I know his title . . . He can be called
a coward . . .
You in the presence of God and in my
presence, hear what I say.

Heavy upon this scoundrel falls a
mighty affliction:
May he be cursed!
(*with terrific force*)
Repeat the malediction!
(*with a sinister look toward Paolo*)

PAOLO (*trembling and terrified*)
May he be cursed!
(*to himself*)
Oh horror! Oh woe!

ALL
May he be cursed!

## ACT TWO

The Doge's apartment in the ducal
palace in Genoa.

*Doors at the sides. The city is seen be-
yond a balcony. A decanter and wine
bowl stand on a table. It is night.*

PAOLO
(*drawing Pietro toward the balcony*)
You saw those two men?

PIETRO
Yes.

PAOLO
Release them quickly from prison,
Take them by that secret passage
Which you may open by this key.

PIETRO
I know it.
(*He goes out.*)

PAOLO
That curse was unexpected!
The malediction hangs on me still.
The air itself is shaken!
I am hated, rejected
By the Senate, by Genoa, as vermin.
Before my flight there is this to do:
determine
The Doge's fate forever,
For he must be broken.
You, who have angered me, although
I crowned you
Here I shall wound you
And fate shall lead you to this hour
of your ruin.
(*He empties a flask which he has
brought into the wine bowl.*)
Here, to kill you I pour a deadly
poison,

Là t'armo un assassino.
Scelga morte sua via
Fra il tosco ed il pugnale.

(*Fiesco e Gabriele condotti da Pietro,
che si ritira.*)

FIESCO
Prigioniero in qual loco m'adduci?

PAOLO
Nelle stanze del Doge, e favella
A te Paolo.

FIESCO
I tuoi sguardi son truci.

PAOLO
Io so l'odio che celasi in te.
Tu m'ascolta.

FIESCO
Che brami?

PAOLO
Al cimento
Preparasti de' Guelfi la schiera?

FIESCO
Sì.

PAOLO
Ma vano fia tanto ardimento!
Questo Doge, abborrito da me
Quanto voi l'abborrite, v'appresta
Nuovo scempio . . .

FIESCO
Mi tendi un agguato.

PAOLO
Un agguato? Di Fiesco la testa
Il tiranno segnata non ha?
Io t'insegno vittoria.

FIESCO
A qual patto?

PAOLO
Trucidarlo qui, mentre egli dorme.

FIESCO
Osi a Fiesco proporre un misfatto?

PAOLO
Tu rifiuti?

FIESCO
Sì.

PAOLO
Al tuo carcer ten va.

(*Fiesco parte; Gabriele fa per seguirlo,
ma è arrestato da Paolo.*)

PAOLO
Udisti?

GABRIELE
Vil disegno!

PAOLO
Amelia dunque mai tu non amasti?

GABRIELE
Che dici?

PAOLO
È qui.

GABRIELE
Qui Amelia!

PAOLO
E del vegliardo
Segno è alle infami dilettanze.

GABRIELE
Astuto demon, cessa . . .

(*Paolo corre a chiuder la
porta di destra.*)

Che fai?

PAOLO
Di qui ogni varco t'è conteso. Ardisci
Il colpo . . . o sepoltura
Avrai fra queste mura.

(*Parte frettoloso dalla porta di
sinistra, che si chiude dietro.*)

GABRIELE
O inferno! Amelia qui! L'ama il
vegliardo!
E il furor che m'accende
M'è conteso sfogar! Tu m'uccidesti
Il padre . . . tu m'involi il mio tesoro . . .
Trema, iniquo . . . già troppa era
un'offesa,
Doppia vendetta hai sul tuo capo
accesa!
Sento avvampar nell'anima
Furente gelosia;
Tutto il mio sangue spegnerle
L'incendio non potria;
S'ei mille vite avesse,
E spegnerle potesse
D'un colpo il mio furor,
Non sarei sazio ancor.
Che parlo! Ahimè! Deliro!
Ah! io piango! Pietà, gran Dio, del
mio martiro!
Cielo pietoso, rendila,
Rendila a questo core,

There, hides an armed assassin.
Death may choose as your portion
Between the drink and dagger.
(*Fiesco and Gabriele are led in by Pietro, who retires.*)

FIESCO

As a prisoner, where do you lead me?

PAOLO

To the Doge's apartments, and you're speaking to Paolo.

FIESCO

Your expression is cruel.

PAOLO

I'm aware of the hate that you feel.
You must hear me.

FIESCO

Then ask me.

PAOLO

Was it you who tried to summon the Guelphs into action?

FIESCO

Yes.

PAOLO

And all of your boldness for nothing?
For this Doge, who is hated by me as by you he is hated,
Is planning further havoc.

FIESCO

You're trying to trap me.

PAOLO

For what reason? The tyrant is waiting
And the axe is all ready for you.
I would help you to triumph.

FIESCO

Your conditions?

PAOLO

That you kill him here, when he is sleeping.

FIESCO

Do you dare to propose this to Fiesco?

PAOLO

You refuse me?

FIESCO

Yes.

PAOLO

Then go back to your cell.
*but is stopped by Paolo.*)
(*Fiesco leaves. Gabriele tries to leave*

PAOLO

You heard us?

GABRIELE

Vile intriguer!

PAOLO

Then it is true you never loved Amelia?

GABRIELE

You mean it?

PAOLO

She's here.

GABRIELE

In the palace?

PAOLO

She is to give the old man his pleasures as a wanton.

GABRIELE

Insidious fiend, stop now.
(*Paolo dashes to bolt the right hand door.*)
What now?

PAOLO

From here every door is closely guarded.
Your hand will strike him
Or you will find your grave within the palace.
(*Paolo hurries out by the left hand door which he fastens behind him.*)

GABRIELE

You devil! Amelia here? She is his mistress!
And the rage that inflames me I'm unable to vent!
You've done to death my father,
You have carried off my treasure . . .
Tremble, tyrant . . .
One crime has got you in trouble,
Once more you trespass, now my revenge is double.
Now blazing with heat my soul's afire
And mad jealousy sears like fever;
All of his blood could hardly quell
The flames that burn forever;
If all his lives were legion;
And to the devil's region
I could consign them with a blow,
All of my torment would not be quelled, ah, no!
What folly! Alas! What madness!
I'm weeping. O God, have pity on my sadness!
Heaven have pity, bring her back,
Bring her back for I adore her,

Pura siccome l'angelo
Che veglia al suo pudore;
Ma se una nube impura
Tanto candor m'oscura,
Priva di sue virtù
Ch'io non la vegga più.

AMELIA

Tu qui?

GABRIELE

Amelia!

AMELIA

Chi il varco t'apria?

GABRIELE

E tu come qui?

AMELIA

Io . . .

GABRIELE

Sleale!

AMELIA

Oh crudele!

GABRIELE

Il tiranno ferale . . .

AMELIA

Il rispetta . . .

GABRIELE

Egli t'ama . . .

AMELIA

D'amor santo!

GABRIELE

E tu?

AMELIA

L'amo del pari.

GABRIELE

E t'ascolto, e non t'uccido?

AMELIA

Infelice! Mel credi, pura io son.

GABRIELE

Favella . . .

AMELIA

Concedi che il segreto non aprasi ancor.

GABRIELE

Parla, in tuo cor virgineo
Fede al diletto rendi.
Il tuo silenzio è funebre
Vel che su me distendi.
Dammi la vita o il feretro,
Sdegno la tua pietà.

AMELIA

Sgombra dall'alma il dubbio . . .
Santa nel petto mio
L'immagin tua s'accoglie
Quale nel tempio Iddio.
No, procellosa tenebra
Un ciel d'amor non ha.

(S'ode uno squillo.)

Il Doge vien. Scampo non hai.
T'ascondi!

GABRIELE

No.

AMELIA

Il patibol t'aspetta!

GABRIELE

Io non lo temo.

AMELIA

All'ora stessa teco avrò morte . . .
Se non ti move di me pietà.

GABRIELE

Di te pietade?

(da sè)

Lo vuol la sorte . . .
Si compia il fato! Egli morrà!

(Amelia nasconde Gabriele sul poggiolo. Il Doge entra leggendo un
foglio.)

DOGE

Figlia!

AMELIA

Sì afflitto, padre mio?

DOGE

T'inganni . . . Ma tu piangevi.

AMELIA

Io?

DOGE

La cagion m'è nota
Delle lagrime tue . . . Già mel
dicesti . . .
Ami; or bene s'è degno
Di te l'eletto del tuo core.

AMELIA

O padre,
Fra i Liguri il più prode, il più
gentile . . .

DOGE

Il noma.

AMELIA

Adorno . . .

DOGE

Il mio nemico!

Pure as the heavenly angel who
Can guard her virtue for her;
But if some dark obscurity
Once should becloud that purity
Which no one can restore,
May I not see her more.

AMELIA

You here?

GABRIELE

Amelia!

AMELIA

Who opened the passage?

GABRIELE

And you . . . by yourself?

AMELIA

I came . . .

GABRIELE

So faithless!

AMELIA

Oh, so cruel!

GABRIELE

That detestable tyrant!

AMELIA

You insult him!

GABRIELE

But he loves you . . .

AMELIA

Love most holy.

GABRIELE

And you?

AMELIA

I love him also.

GABRIELE

At your words I'd like to kill you.

AMELIA

Oh, unhappy, believe me, I am pure.

GABRIELE

Then tell me.

AMELIA

Then swear to keep a secret that no
one may hear!

GABRIELE

Speak from your heart, so pure, so dear
And nevermore deceive me,
Over my head your silence is hanging,
An ominous evil to grieve me.
Give me assurance, give life to me or
death to me,
Pity from you I shall spurn.

AMELIA

Cleanse from your heart all doubt
of me,
My love is pure and simple
I worship you in my heart,
A godhead within his temple.
All of the storms that cloud the sky
From love's domain shall turn.
(flourish of trumpets)
The Doge is there. You cannot flee.
Go quickly.

GABRIELE

No.

AMELIA

But the scaffold is waiting!

GABRIELE

I do not fear it.

AMELIA

Then I shall perish beside my lover
If nothing moves you to pity me.

GABRIELE

You ask my pity?
His life is over.
(to himself)
For fate demands it and he must die.
(Amelia hides Gabriele on the balcony.
The Doge enters, reading a paper.)

DOGE

Daughter!

AMELIA

You're sad, beloved father?

DOGE

No matter . . . But you were weeping.

AMELIA

Weeping?

DOGE

I can guess the reason for your
weeping, my daughter,
For there is someone you love; be
happy,
If he is the man who's good enough
to win you.

AMELIA

O father, the bravest in Liguria
And the most courtly.

DOGE

Who is he?

AMELIA

Adorno . . .

DOGE

He is a traitor!

AMELIA
Padre!

DOGE
Vedi: qui scritto il nome suo?
Congiura coi Guelfi!

AMELIA
Ciel! Perdonagli!

DOGE
Nol posso.

AMELIA
Con lui morrò.

DOGE
L'ami cotanto?

AMELIA
L'amo d'ardente, d'infinito amor. O al
tempio
Con lui mi guida, o sovra entrambi
cada
La scure del carnefice . . .

DOGE
O crudele destino!
O dileguate mie speranze!
Una figlia ritrovo; ed un nemico
A me la invola! Ascolta:
S'ei ravveduto . . .

AMELIA
Il fia . . .

DOGE
Forse il perdono allor . . .

AMELIA
Padre adorato!

DOGE
Ti ritraggi . . .
Attender qui degg'io l'aurora.

AMELIA
Lascia ch'io vegli al tuo fianco.

DOGE
No, ti ritraggi.

AMELIA
Padre!

DOGE
Il voglio.

AMELIA
(escendo a sinistra)
Gran Dio! Come salvarlo?

DOGE
Doge! Ancor proveran la tua clemenza
I traditori? Di paura segno
Fora il castigo. M'ardono le fauci.
(Versa dall'anfora nella
tazza e beve.)
Perfin l' acqua del fonte è amara al
labbro
Dell'uom che regna! O duol! La mente
è oppressa. . .
(Siede.)
Stanche le membra . . . ohimè! . . . mi
vince il sonno.
O Amelia . . . ami un nemico!
(S'addormenta. Gabrielle entra con
precauzione, s'avvicina al Doge e lo
contempla.)

GABRIELE
Ei dorme! Quale
Sento ritegno? È riverenza o tema?
Vacilla il mio voler? Tu dormi, o
veglio,
Del padre mio carnefice, tu mio
Rival . . . Figlio d'Adorno! La paterna
Ombra ti chiama vindice.
(Brandisce un pugnale e va per trafig-
gere il Doge, ma Amelia, che era
ritornata, va rapidamente a porsi tra
esso ed il padre.)

AMELIA
Insensato!
Vecchio inerme il tuo braccio colpisce?

GABRIELE
Tua difesa mio sdegno raccende.

AMELIA
Santo, id giuro, è l'amor che ci unisce,
Nè alle nostre speranze contende.

GABRIELE
Che favelli?

DOGE (destandosi)
Ah!

AMELIA
Father!

DOGE
See how his name leads all the others?
He heads the rebellion.

AMELIA
God forgive them all!

DOGE
I cannot.

AMELIA
Have mercy.

DOGE
I cannot.

AMELIA
Then I must die.

DOGE
You love him so much?

AMELIA
My heart is burning with the passion
of love.
Oh lead us before the altar or order
our execution,
We shall die together and meet a
common punishment . . .

DOGE
Oh, the fates can be cruel!
How I can see my hopes dissolving!
I recover a daughter and my foe must
take her from me!
But listen, if he is contrite . . .

AMELIA
He will be.

DOGE
I might forgive him then . . .

AMELIA
Father, I love you!

DOGE
You must leave me.
I shall wait here until the morning.

AMELIA
I'll stay here, watching beside you . . .

DOGE
No, you must leave me.

AMELIA
Father!

DOGE
I wish it.

AMELIA (leaving at the left)
Oh heavens, how can I save him?

DOGE
Once more as Doge must I prove to
all the traitors
I am lenient? If I punish them
It might seem I feared them. I am
feeling thirsty.
(He empties the decanter into the
goblet and drinks.)
Even water is bitter on the tongue to
the man who governs!
Alas, my mind is weary.
(He sinks on a chair.)
My limbs are tired . . . Alas, sleep has
overcome me.
(He sleeps.)
Amelia, you love that Adorno!
(Gabriele enters cautiously, approaches
the Doge and watches him.)

GABRIELE
He's sleeping. Why am I so reluctant?
Is it from awe or terror? Or have I
lost my will?
Old man, you're sleeping, my blessed
father's murderer!
Rival to me, son of Adorno whose
most tragic death
His own son must vindicate.
(Brandishing a dagger he is about to
stab the Doge when Amelia, return-
ing, hurries between the two men.)

AMELIA
Would you strike him,
An old man, when he cannot defend
him?

GABRIELE
Your defense is arousing me slowly.

AMELIA
But the love that unites us is holy,
And will help us, if you comprehend
him.

GABRIELE
Comprehend him?

DOGE (waking)
Ah!

AMELIA
Nascondi il pugnale,
Vien . . . ch'ei t'oda.

GABRIELE
Prostrarmi al suo piede?

AMELIA
Vien!

DOGE
(dirigendosi a Gabriele)
Ecco il petto . . . colpisci, sleale!

GABRIELE
Sangue il sangue d'Adorno ti chiede.

DOGE
E fia ver? Chi t'apria queste porte?

AMELIA
Non io.

GABRIELE
Niun quest'arcano saprà.

DOGE
Il dirai fra tormenti . . .

GABRIELE
La morte,
Tuoi supplizi non temo.

AMELIA
Ah pietà!

DOGE
Ah! Quel padre tu ben vendicasti,
Che da me contristato già fu . . .
Un celeste tesor m'involasti
La mia figlia.

GABRIELE
Suo padre sei tu!
Perdon, Amelia. Indomito,
Geloso amor fu il mio.
Doge, il velame squarciasi!
Un assassin son io!
Dammi la morte; il ciglio
A te non oso alzar.

AMELIA
Madre, che dall'empireo
Proteggi la tua figlia,
Del genitore all'anima
Meco pietà consiglia!
Ei si rendea colpevole
Solo per troppo amor!

DOGE
Deggio salvarlo e stendere
La mano all'inimico?
Sì, pace splenda ai Liguri,
Si plachi l'odio antico,
Sia d'amistanze italiche
Il mio sepolcro altar.

CORO
All'armi, all'armi, o Liguri,
Sacro dover v'appella
Scoppiò dell'ira il folgore;
È notte di procella.

AMELIA
(corre alla finestra)
Quai gridi?

GABRIELE (a Doge)
I tuoi nemici . . .

DOGE
Il so.

AMELIA
S'addensa il popolo.

DOGE
(a Gabriele)
Va! T'unisci a' tuoi!

CORO
Le guelfe spade cingano
Di tirannia lo spalto;
Del coronato demone,
Su, alla magion, l'assalto.

GABRIELE (a Doge)
Ch'io pugni contro di te? Mai più.

DOGE
Dunque messaggio
Ti reca lor di pace,
E il sole di domani
Non sorga a rischiarar fraterne stragi.

GABRIELE
Teco a pugnar ritorno,
Se la clemenza tua non li disarmi.

DOGE
(accennando Amelia)
Sarà costei tuo premio.

GABRIELE E AMELIA
Oh! Inaspettata gioia!

AMELIA
Padre!

DOGE, GABRIELE E CORO
All'armi!

AMELIA

Your sword must be hidden, come
address him . . .

GABRIELE

Must I kneel before him?

AMELIA

Come.

DOGE (to Gabriele)

Here's your target, now strike me,
you traitor!

GABRIELE

Blood for blood is the cry of Adorno.

DOGE

Is it true? Who permitted you to
enter?

AMELIA

Not I, sir.

GABRIELE

That man will never be known.

DOGE

You will speak under torture . . .

GABRIELE

I fear not either torture or murder.

AMELIA

Oh, my God.

DOGE

Ah, your vengeance is filled in full
measure
For the man I attacked as his due.
You have stolen a heavenly treasure:
My own daughter . . .

GABRIELE

Her father—are you?
Forgive, forgive, Amelia.
My love for you was raging with
jealous passion.
Sire, the confusion melts away.
I am so vile, I am a vile assassin.
You may condemn me, I dare not face
your judgment,
I dare not raise my eyes to yours, I
dare not see.

AMELIA

Mother in heaven above me, I pray
for your protection.
Grant to my father pity to mingle with
his affection . . .
He whom I love is culpable only
through love of me.

DOGE

Should I forgive my enemy, admit
him to my favor?
Yes, to placate Liguria, my purpose
cannot waver.
There must be peace in Italy, though
on my grave it shall be.

CHORUS

To arms, Ligurians, to arms!
Your sacred duties call you!
The bolts of wrath have struck again,
But night shall not appall you.

AMELIA (running to the balcony)

What shouting!

GABRIELE (to the Doge)

Your foes are coming.

DOGE

I know.

AMELIA

The crowd is thickening.

DOGE (to Gabriele)

Go and join your own men.

CHORUS

Battle! Destruction!
The Guelphs gird on their swords
today
To curb the tyrant's malice.
Let us destroy the devil's crown
And raze the Doge's palace.

GABRIELE (to the Doge)

Can I then, fight against you? No
more.

DOGE

Go then as spokesman
And try to pacify them,
So that the sun, tomorrow,
May not arise to light the strife of
brothers.

GABRIELE

I will fight here beside you
If mercy still at length will not disarm
them.

DOGE (pointing to Amelia)

Your prize will be Amelia.

GABRIELE AND AMELIA

Oh, what happiness unbounded!

AMELIA

Father!

DOGE, GABRIELE AND CHORUS

To battle!

## ATTO TERZO
Interno del Palazzo Ducale.

*Di prospetto grandi aperture dalle
quali si scorgerà Genova illuminata a
festa: in fondo il mare:*

GRIDA (*interne*)

Evviva il Doge! Vittoria! Vittoria!

CAPITANO DEI BALESTRIERI

(*rimettendo a Fiesco la sua spada*)

Libero sei. Ecco la spada.

FIESCO

E i Guelfi?

CAPITANO

Sconfitti.

FIESCO

O triste libertà!
Che? Paolo?
Dove sei tratto?

PAOLO (*arrestandosi*)

All'estremo supplizio.
Il mio demonio mi cacciò fra l'armi
Del rivoltosi e là fui côlto; ed ora
Mi condanna Simon; ma da me prima
Fu il Boccanegra condannato a morte.

FIESCO

Che vuoi dir?

PAOLO

Un velen, (più nulla io temo)
Gli divora la vita.

FIESCO

Infame!

PAOLO

Ei forse già mi precede nell'avel!

CORO (*interno*)

Dal sommo delle sfere
Proteggili, Signor;
Di pace sien foriere
Le nozze dell'amor.

PAOLO

Ah, orrore!
Quel canto nuzïal, che mi persegue,
L'odi? In quel tempio Gabriele
   Adorno
Sposa colei ch'io trafugava!

FIESCO

(*sguainando la spada*)

Amelia?
Tu fosti il rapitor? Mostro!

PAOLO

Ferisci.

FIESCO

Non lo sperar; sei sacro alla bipenne.

(*Le guardie transcinano Paolo.*)

Inorridisco! No, Simon, non questa
Vendetta chiesi, d'altra meta degno
Era il tuo fato. Eccolo il Doge.
Alfine è giunta l'ora di trovarci a
   fronte!

(*Si ritira in un angolo d'ombra. Entra
il Capitano con un trombettiere.*)

CAPITANO (*al verone*)

Cittadini! per ordine del Doge
S'estinguano le faci e non s'offenda
Col clamor del trionfo i prodi estinti.

(*Esce seguito dal trombettiere.*)

DOGE (*entra*)

M'ardon le tempia . . . un'atra vampa
   sento
Serpeggiar per le vene! Ah! ch'io
   respiri
L'aura beata del libero cielo!
Oh refrigerio! La marina brezza!
Il mare! Quale in rimirarlo
Di glorie e di sublimi rapimenti
Mi affaccian ricordi! Il mar!
   Il mar!
Ah perchè in suo grembo non trovai la
   tomba?

FIESCO (*avvicinandosi*)

Era meglio per te!

DOGE

Chi osò inoltrarsi?

## ACT THREE

The Doge's apartment in the ducal palace.

*Through a great window lies Genoa, lighted for a festival; in the background the sea.*

VOICES (*within*)

Long live our monarch, our victor, our victor!

CAPTAIN OF THE ARCHERS

(*returning the sword to Fiesco*)

Now you are free. Here is your weapon.

FIESCO

The Guelphs, then?

CAPTAIN

Defeated.

FIESCO

Their liberty is sad!
What? Paolo? Where do they take you?

PAOLO (*standing*)

To my own execution.
An evil fate pursued me to the army of the insurgents.
There I was captured: and Simon has condemned me to die:
But I have first condemned Boccanegra that he too may perish.

FIESCO

Tell me more!

PAOLO

There's a drug (I now fear nothing) he has drunk and is dying.

FIESCO

You villain!

PAOLO

Perhaps he now will precede me to my death!

CHORUS (*within*)

May God above be shedding
His grace, on Him we call.
And may this happy wedding
Betoken peace for all.

PAOLO

Ah, how dreadful!
The echo of that hymn, how it pursues me.
Listen, in that chapel Gabriele Adorno
Marries the girl whom I abducted . . .

FIESCO (*unsheathing his sword*)

Amelia! Were you the wicked man? Monster!

PAOLO

Then strike me.

FIESCO

No hope for you! We'll keep you for the scaffold.

(*The guards drag Paolo away.*)

FIESCO

I'm filled with horror!
No, Simon, this vengeance was not my doing.
You deserved another fate as your portion.
Here he is, our Simon. At last the hour is striking.
We can face each other.

(*He retires into a shadowy corner. The Captain enters, with a trumpeter.*)

CAPTAIN

(*addressing the people from the balcony*)

Hear my tidings! The Doge has given orders:
You will put out your torches
And not offend the heroes lying before you
With shouts of triumph.

(*He leaves, followed by the trumpeter.*)

DOGE (*entering*)

Fever destroys me. An evil fire is burning,
Through my veins it is coursing.
Would I were breathing those blessed breezes
From wide open spaces. Oh, how refreshing!
Breezes from the seashore!
The ocean! The ocean! Gazing at the billows,
My memories of glory and of rapture
Are forever returning.
The sea! The sea!
Ah, but why, why could I not find
My grave within your bosom?

FIESCO (*approaching*)

It were better for you!

DOGE

Who has dared to enter?

FIESCO
Chi te non teme.

DOGE
Guardie?

FIESCO
Invan le appelli.
Non son qui i sgherri tuoi.
M'ucciderai, ma pria m'odi.

DOGE
Che vuoi?

FIESCO
Delle faci festanti al barlume
Cifre arcane, funebri vedrai . . .
Tua sentenza lamano del nume
Sovra queste pareti vergò.
Di tua stella s'eclissano i rai:
La tua porpora in brani già cade;
Vincitor tra le larve morrai
Cui la tomba tua scure negò!

(*I lumi della città e del porto comin-
ciano a spegnersi.*)

DOGE
Quale accento?

FIESCO
Lo udisti un'altra volta.

DOGE
Fia ver? Risorgon dalle tombe i morti?

FIESCO
Non mi ravvisi tu?

DOGE
Fiesco!

FIESCO
Simone, morti ti salutano!

DOGE
Gran Dio!
Compito è alfin di quest'alma il desio!

FIESCO
Come fantasima Fiesco t'appar,
Antico oltraggio a vendicar.

DOGE
Di pace nunzio Fiesco sarà,
Suggella un angelo nostra amistà.

FIESCO
Che dici?

DOGE
Un tempo il tuo perdon m'offristi.

FIESCO
Io?

DOGE
Se a te l'orfanella concedea
Che perduta per sempre allor piangea.
In Amelia Grimaldi a me fu resa,
E il nome porta della madre estinta.

FIESCO
Ceil! Perchè mi splende il ver sì tardi?

DOGE
Tu piangi! Perchè volgi altrove il
　　　ciglio?

FIESCO
Piango, perchè mi parla
In te del ciel la voce;
Sento rampogna atroce
Fin nella tu pietà.

DOGE
Vien, ch'io ti stringa al petto,
O padre di Maria;
Balsamo all'alma mia
Il tuo perdon sarà.

FIESCO
Ohimè! morte sovrasta . . . un traditore
Il velén t'apprestò.

DOGE
Tutto favella,
Il sento, in me d'eternità.

FIESCO
Crudele fato!

DOGE
Ella vien!

FIESCO
Maria . . .

DOGE
Taci, non dirle.
Anco una volta vo' benedirla.

(*S'abbandona sopra un seggiolone.
Amelia, Gabriele, Senatori, Dame,
Gentiluomini, Paggi con torce.*)

FIESCO

A man who fears not.

DOGE

Guardsmen!

FIESCO

In vain you call them, for your men
    are not there.
I may be dead, but first hear me.

DOGE

Then speak!

FIESCO

Where the torches are joyfully glowing,
You will soon see the glory is shaded,
And the fate that the gods are
    bestowing
Will be written for you on the wall.
For the light of your star now has faded
And the purple is fallen to tatters,
Only ghosts will acclaim you as Doge,
For whom the tomb is the realm of
    your fall.

(*The lights are gradually extinguished
    in the city.*)

DOGE

Who is speaking?

FIESCO

A voice from days long ended.

DOGE

How so? Do men rise up from death to
    haunt us?

FIESCO

You do not know my face?

DOGE

Fiesco!

FIESCO

Simone, the dead rise up to speak
    with you.

DOGE

Great heaven! At last the wish of my
    soul has been granted!

FIESCO

Ghost from another world, Fiesco
    appears,
Vengeance for outrage, ancient outrage
    across the years.

DOGE

Peace is the message Fiesco will bear.
Angels will seal the pact, love we shall
    share.

FIESCO

Your meaning?

DOGE

Long since you offered me your
    pardon . . .

FIESCO

Did I?

DOGE

If I would give up the little orphan
Who was lost, so I thought as I
    lamented.
In Amelia Grimaldi I have found her,
Though she bears the name her mother
    gave her.

FIESCO

God! But why was light so long in
    coming?

DOGE

You're weeping!
Ah, but why do your eyes avoid me?

FIESCO

I weep, because I hear you:
A voice from heaven winging;
Cruel remorse is stinging
Just because you are so good.

DOGE

Come, let me hold you closer,
Maria's loving father.
'Tis balm to heal me, rather
As your forgiveness would.

FIESCO

Alas, death is the master,
An evil wretch brewed the poison for
    you.

DOGE

Everything tells me, I feel it,
That I am near the end.

FIESCO

Oh fate is cruel!

DOGE

She is here . . .

FIESCO

Maria.

DOGE

Silence, keep silence . . .
For one last time I long, long to bless
    her.

(*He sinks on his throne as Amelia and
    Gabriele come in with the Senators
    and ladies and gentlemen of the
    court. Pages bear torches.*)

AMELIA
(*vedendo Fiesco*)
Chi veggo!

DOGE
Vien . . .

GABRIELE (*tra sè*)
Fiesco!

AMELIA (*a Fiesco*)
Tu qui!

DOGE
Deponi la meraviglia.
In Fiesco il padre vedi
Dell'ignota Maria, che ti die' vita.

AMELIA
Egli? Fia ver?

FIESCO
Maria!

AMELIA
Oh gioia! Allora
Gli odi funesti han fine!

DOGE
Tutto finisce, o figlia!

AMELIA
Qual ferale
Pensier t'attrista sì sereni istanti?

DOGE
Maria, coraggio . . . A gran dolor
t'appresta.

AMELIA E GABRIELE
Quali accenti! Oh terror!

DOGE
Per me l'estrema ora suonò!
(*sorpresa generale*)

AMELIA E GABRIELE
Che parli?

DOGE
Ma l'Eterno
In tue braccia, o Maria,
Mi concede a spirar.

AMELIA E GABRIELE
(*cadendo a piedi del Doge*)
Possibil fia?

DOGE
(*sorge, e imponendo sul loro capo le
mani, solleva gli occhi al cielo*)
Gran Dio, li benedici
Pietosó dall'empiro;
A lor del mio martiro
Cangia le spine in fior.

AMELIA
No, non morrai, l'amore
Vinca di morte il gelo,
Risponderà dal cielo
Pietade al mio dolor.

GABRIELE
O padre, o padre, il seno
Furia mi squarcia atroce.
Come passò veloce
L'ora del lieto amor.!

FIESCO
Ogni letizia in terra
È menzognero incanto,
D'interminato pianto
Fonte è l'umano cor.

DOGE
T'appressa, o figlia . . . io spiro . . .
Stringi . . . il morente . . al cor!

CORO
Sì, piange è ver,
Piange ognor la creatura;
Si avvolge la natura
In manto di dolor!

DOGE
Senatori! Sancite il voto estremo.
(*I Senatori s'appressano.*)
Questo serto ducal la fronte cinga
Di Gabriele Adorno.
Tu, Fiesco, compi il mio voler . . .
Maria!
(*Spira.*)

AMELIA E GABRIELE
(*s'inginocchiano davanti al cadavere*)
Padre!

FIESCO
(*s'avvicina al verone circondato dai
Senatori e Paggi, che alzano
le fiaccole*)
Genovesi! In Gabriele
Adorno il vostro Doge or acclamate.

VOCI (*dalla piazza*)
No . . . Boccanegra!

FIESCO
È morto . . .
Pace per lui pregate!

CORO
Pace per lui!
(*Tutti s'inginocchiano.*)

FINE DELL' OPERA

AMELIA (*seeing Fiesco*)
Who is it?

DOGE
Come!

GABRIELE (*aside*)
Fiesco!

AMELIA (*to Fiesco*)
You here?

DOGE
His coming need not surprise you.
For Fiesco is the father of the unknown
 Maria
Who was your mother.

AMELIA
And this is true?

FIESCO
Maria!

AMELIA
How joyous the tidings!
All of the feuds are over.

DOGE
It all is finished, daughter!

AMELIA
What a sorrowful thought
To darken such a happy moment!

DOGE
Maria, have courage, prepare for tragic
 sorrow.

AMELIA AND GABRIELE
Fateful accents! I'm afraid.

DOGE
For me the final hour is at hand!
(*general consternation*)

AMELIA AND GABRIELE
Have pity!

DOGE
But Maria, in your arms,
God has granted that I may breathe
 my last.

AMELIA AND GABRIELE
(*falling at the Doge's feet*)
Is death so certain?

DOGE
(*rising, placing his hands on their heads
 and raising his eyes to heaven*)
O God in heaven, bless them,
For them my soul is crying.
The crown I leave them, dying—
Change all its thorns to flowers.

AMELIA
You shall not die, for loving
Conquers the bleakness of dying,
Heaven will be replying
With all its blessed powers.

GABRIELE
O father, bitter anguish
My very soul is tearing.
Brief was the joy of sharing
All the love that once was ours.

FIESCO
The joys that earth can offer,
Pleasures are always lying.
The human heart is crying
All of its waking hours.

DOGE
Come to me, daughter, I'm dying,
Hold me, hold me closer,
Hold me near your heart.

CHORUS
All of us weep,
Sorrowful creatures,
We clothe our human natures
In weeping, soothe the heart.

DOGE
May the Senate fulfill my final promise.
Place the crown of the Doge
Upon the head of Gabriele Adorno.
And Fiesco, carry out my wish. Maria!
(*He dies.*)

AMELIA AND GABRIELE
(*kneeling before his body*)
Father! Father!

FIESCO
(*He walks to the balcony, followed by
 the Senators and pages with their
 torches raised.*)
Men of Genoa! In Gabriele Adorno
 you have a Doge, you may acclaim
 him.

VOICES (*from the square*)
No, Boccanegra!

FIESCO
He is dead. Pray for his soul in heaven.
(*All kneel.*)

CHORUS
Peace be with him.

END OF THE OPERA